United States Coast Guard

BRUNO LURCH

Heinemann Library
Chicago, Illinois

© 2004 Heinemann Library,
a division of Reed Elsevier Inc.
Chicago, Illinois

Customer Service 888-454-2279

Visit our website at www.heinemannlibrary.com

Series design by Heinemann Library
Page layout by Malcolm Walker
Photo research by Bill Broyles
Printed and bound in China by
    WKT Company Limited.

08 07 06 05 04
10 9 8 7 6 5 4 3 2 1

Library of Congress Cataloging-in-Publication Data

Lurch, Bruno, 1956-
  United States Coast Guard / Bruno Lurch.
    p. cm. -- (U.S. Armed Forces)
Includes bibliographical references and index.
  ISBN 1-4034-4550-8 (hardcover) -- ISBN 1-4034-4556-7
(pbk.)
  1. United States. Coast Guard--Juvenile literature. [1.
United States.
Coast Guard.] I. Title. II. U.S. Armed Forces (Series)
  VG53.L87 2004
  363.28'6'0973--dc22
                    2003023784

Produced for Heinemann Library by
White-Thomson Publishing Ltd
2/3 St Andrew's Place
Lewes UK   BN7 1UP

Acknowledgments
The author and publisher are grateful to the following for
permission to reproduce copyright material:
Title page, contents page, pp. 4, 5, 6, 7, 8, 9, 10, 11, 12, 13,
14, 15, 16, 17, U.S. Coast Guard; p. 18t, Library of
Congress; pp. 18b, 19, 20, U.S. Coast Guard; p. 21t, Women
in Military Service for America Memorial Foundation; pp.
21b, 22, U.S. Coast Guard; p. 23, National Archives and
Records Administration; pp. 24, 25, U.S. Coast Guard; p.26,
Defense Visual Information Center; pp, 27, 28, 29, 30, 31,
32, 33, 34, 35, 36, 37, 38, 39, 40, 41, 42, 43, 44, 45, U.S.
Coast Guard.
Cover photograph by James A. Sugar.

Every effort has been made to contact copyright holders of
any material reproduced in this book. Any omissions will be
rectified in subsequent printings if notice is given to the
publisher.

Special thanks to Lt. Col. G.A. Lofaro for his review of this
book.

Note to the Reader: Some words are shown in bold,
like this. You can find out what they mean by
looking in the glossary.

Contents

What Is the Coast Guard?

The United States Coast Guard was formed from five separate departments. These included the Lighthouse Service, the **Revenue Cutter** Service, the Steamboat Inspection Service, the Bureau of **Navigation**, and the Life Saving Service. The Lighthouse Service is the oldest one. The United States Congress established it in 1789.

In 1915 President Woodrow Wilson signed an order that set up the Coast Guard. At that time, it included only the Revenue Cutter Service and the Life-Saving Service. By 1946, all five departments were part of the U.S. Coast Guard.

A Coast Guard cutter patrols off the coast of Alaska.

5 Original Departments of the Coast Guard

The Lighthouse Service established August 1789	to build, operate, and maintain lighthouses and sea markers in U.S. coastal waters
The Revenue Cutter Service established August 1790	to organize the enforcement of customs regulations
The Steamboat Inspection Service established August 1852	to enforce laws relative to the construction, safety, operation, equipment inspection, and documentation of merchant vessels. Investigates marine casualties.
The Life Saving Service established June 1878	to establish and maintain life saving stations along the coasts of the United States
The Bureau of Navigation established July 1884	to administer and enforce navigation laws

The Coast Guard is the fifth branch of the armed services. However, most of the time it performs nonmilitary peacetime duties.

The main job of the United States Coast Guard is to support national security. It does this by protecting the public, the environment, and the country's business interests in **maritime** regions. The modern Coast Guard uses many different types of aircraft and seagoing vehicles.

During a typical day, United States Coast Guard members will save lives through search-and-rescue missions. They will protect millions of dollars in property. They will capture as much as 500 pounds (227 kilograms) of illegal drugs. They will help clean up a dozen or more dangerous chemical spills.

Protecting the Coast

The Coast Guard works to protect more than 95,000 miles (153,000 kilometers) of the United States' coastlines. This area includes ports, harbors, and inland waterways. These areas are in the United States, Puerto Rico, and on some Pacific islands. The Coast Guard also patrols and protects international waterways that total close to 3.5 million square miles (9 million square kilometers).

A Coast Guard fire team fights a fishing boat fire off Miami, Florida.

The Coast Guard cutter *Boutwell* patrols the North Arabian Sea in 2003.

The main seagoing vehicle of the Coast Guard is called a **cutter**. Cutters of the early 1800s were simple boats with a few pieces of equipment. Today's cutter is a high-tech vessel with state-of-the-art equipment.

The Revenue cutter *Eagle* captures a French vessel in the West Indies in 1799.

The First Cutters

The first seven United States Coast Guard cutters were placed on **active duty** in 1791. They were the *Vigilant, Active, General Green, Massachusetts, Scammel, Argus,* and *Virginia*. All were built in the United States. They were stationed along the east coast, in ports as far north as New Hampshire and as far south as Virginia.

Harry G. Hamlet's long career in the Coast Guard began in 1894, when he was a cadet. His first assignment was on an expedition to the Arctic in 1897–1898 that rescued the crews of four whaling vessels.

The Coast Guard Creed

Every Coast Guard member knows the Creed of the United States Coast Guard. The creed was written in 1938 by Vice Admiral Harry G. Hamlet, commandant of the United States Coast Guard from 1932 to 1936. The Coast Guard officially adopted it in 1950.

Here is the first part of the creed "I am proud to be a United States Coast Guardsman. I revere [respect] that long line of expert seamen who by their devotion to duty and sacrifice of self have made it possible for me to be a member of a service honored and respected, in peace and in war, throughout the world. . . ."

Know It

The United States Coast Guard motto is *Semper paratus*. The words are Latin for "Always ready." It is similar to "Be prepared," the motto of the Boy Scouts and Girl Scouts.

Who Can Join the Coast Guard?

To join the Coast Guard, a person must either be a United States citizen or a resident alien (someone born in another country who has permission to live in the United States). The person must be between the ages of 17 and 27, and must have a high school diploma. The person may have no more than two dependents (people, such as children, who need that person for support). A person must also pass a medical exam. He or she may sign up for two, three, four, or six years at a time. A person who joins the Coast Guard in this way is called an **enlistee**.

People who want to join the Coast Guard, or any branch of the United States Armed Forces, must pass a test called the Armed Services Vocational Aptitude Battery (ASVAB). This test helps determine if people qualify for military service and, if so, what jobs they can do. The test measures knowledge of the English language, math, general science, automobile mechanics, and other special skills. Along with the test results, an applicant's personal interests, school grades, and accomplishments are considered.

Coast Guard cadets learn to use sextants to determine their position on the Earth.

Paid College Tuition

A law known as the Montgomery GI Bill provides money to pay for college tuition or job training for Coast Guard members. The GI bill offers a Coast Guard member up to $28,000 in return for a $1,200 contribution. So for a payment of $100 per month for one year, a Coast Guard member can receive enough money to pay for college tuition.

SPARs trained with pistols during World War II (1941–1945)

SPARS

The Coast Guard Women's Reserve, known as SPARS, was created in 1942. The term SPARS comes from the Coast Guard's Latin motto, *Semper paratus*. During World War II, more than 10,000 women volunteered to join SPARS. They helped protect the nation's shoreline. The first SPAR to be sworn into the regular Coast Guard was Alice Jefferson in 1973.

Those interested in attending Officer Candidate School must be 21 years old and have a college degree. Or they must have military experience and several college courses. Only U.S. citizens can be officers.

Coast Guard members receive a salary and health insurance. They also have vacation benefits and can get promotions for good job performance. **Recruits** can also get up to $12,000 when they sign up.

A Coast Guard petty officer takes the helm, or steers the ship.

Women in the Coast Guard

About one out of every ten Coast Guard members is a woman. All positions in the Coast Guard are open to women. Women have reached the highest ranks in the Coast Guard, including commanders and executive officers.

Training for the Coast Guard

Boot camp is where new **recruits** learn the skills necessary to be a member of the Coast Guard. It takes place at the Coast Guard Training Center at Cape May, New Jersey. Each recruit is assigned to a large group called a company. There are between 50 and 60 recruits in each company. A company commander is in charge. Boot camp lasts eight weeks.

Boot camp is physically and mentally challenging. Recruits must learn water survival, how to use weapons, how to provide first aid, and how to operate radios.

Recruits yell during a physical fitness drill at boot camp in Cape May, New Jersey.

Choosing a Job

Recruits can choose from a variety of jobs in the Coast Guard. These include **radar** operator, health services technician, and marine science technician. After they leave the Coast Guard, men and women can use their skills to get **civilian** jobs such as air traffic controller, missile tracking specialist, X-ray technician, and computer technician. Recruits who have a college degree may go to Officer Candidate School. This is a seventeen-week program that is offered at the Coast Guard Reserve Training Center, in Yorktown, Virginia. Graduates earn **commissions** as Coast Guard officers.

Coast Guard Academy

Instead of enlisting in the Coast Guard, a man or woman can apply to the Coast Guard Academy in New London, Connecticut. The academy is a four-year university. To enroll in the academy, a student must have a high school diploma, good grades, and high test scores. A student at the academy is called a cadet.

Cadets take regular college courses at the Coast Guard Academy. They also receive special officer's training. Graduates of the Coast Guard Academy earn a college degree and an officer's rank. They may then serve as a junior officer aboard a Coast Guard ship.

Students at the Coast Guard Academy raise and lower the flag each day.

Academy Sports

Sports and athletics are important at the Coast Guard Academy. Cadets may choose from 23 sports—11 for men, 9 for women, and 3 for both men and women. These include football, baseball, tennis, golf, soccer, basketball, volleyball, and rowing.

Coast Guard Jobs

Coast Guard jobs are interesting and challenging. Some jobs also require passing twelve- to twenty-week-long courses at Coast Guard training centers called A-schools. After completing a term with the Coast Guard, an **enlistee** can find related jobs in the **civilian** world. Here are four of the many Coast Guard jobs:

Boatswain's Mate (BM)

BMs operate cranes to load supplies, stand watch for security, and manage deck crews. BMs serve as officers in charge of patrol boats and search-and-rescue stations.

Being a BM can help lead to the following jobs in civilian life:

pier superintendent   marina supervisor
tugboat crewman   marina operator
heavy equipment operator   ship pilot

A boatswain's mate circles an oil tanker while a crew searches the vessel.

Electronics Technician (ET)

ETs maintain and repair electronics equipment, radio receivers, transmitters, **radar, navigation** equipment, and computer equipment.

Being an ET can lead to the following jobs in civilian life:

electronics technician   computer technician
guidance systems specialist   telephone repair
radio and radar repair

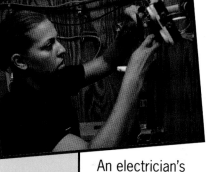

An electrician's mate student works on a panel in class.

Aviation Survival Technician (AST)

ASTs repair aircraft. They perform aircraft inspections and aviation administrative duties. ASTs are also **helicopter** rescue swimmers and emergency medical technicians (EMTs).

ASTs perform thrilling rescues, such as saving people during hurricanes and from ships stranded far out at sea. Sometimes these missions involve helicopters. For these missions, ASTs are lowered from a helicopter to the deck of the stranded or sinking ship. Then they grab the people, one by one, and carry them back to the helicopter.

An AST student learns how to rescue someone in the water.

Being an AST can help lead to the following jobs in civilian life:
land and water survival instructor
parachute rigging and repair
life support equipment technician
commercial aircraft life support technician
paramedic

Radarman

Radarmen—who might be men or women—are the Coast Guard's information experts. They operate computers, radar, and satellite systems. Radarmen make sure ships can use **data** in computer networks for safe navigation. They receive information over global **communication** systems. They collect data that can be used to help Coast Guard units catch criminals and rescue people at sea.

Being a radarman can lead to the following jobs in civilian life:
air traffic controller
control room manager
radio operator
imagery analyst
intelligence analyst

A radarman tracks ships off the Iraqi coast in 2003.

Coast Guard Ships and Boats

The Coast Guard keeps a fleet of small boats and large ships. Different types of ships and boats handle the wide variety of Coast Guard jobs. The main vessel is the **cutter**. A cutter is any ship longer than 65 feet (20 meters)—about the length of two school buses parked end to end. Cutters have living quarters for crew members. Larger cutters also carry smaller boats that can travel where the larger cutters cannot go.

Types of cutters

The largest cutters are the Polar Class icebreakers. These are strong ships that can break through ice-covered water. These giants stretch up to 399 feet (122 meters) in length—that's about the length of one and one-half football fields. The Coast Guard has two Polar Class icebreakers. They work in the freezing ice-covered seas around the North and South Poles. Their crews do scientific research and deliver supplies to research stations in hard-to-reach areas such as Antarctica.

The Coast Guard's twelve High Endurance cutters are only a little smaller than the Polar Class icebreakers. These ships have **helicopter** landing pads and hangars where helicopters can be stored. They perform a variety of missions throughout the world's oceans.

This High Endurance cutter was on duty in the North Arabian Gulf during the Iraqi war in 2003.

Deployable pursuit boats take part in training exercises.

Types of Coast Guard boats

Any Coast Guard vessel shorter than 65 feet is classified as a boat. The Coast Guard has about 1,400 boats. Boats usually operate near shorelines and on inland waterways, such as lakes and rivers. Lifeboats with motors range in length from 44 to 52 feet (13.4 to 15.8 meters). These sturdy boats can sail in the roughest, stormiest seas and are nearly impossible to sink. They are used mostly for rescue work.

Deployable Pursuit Boats are designed for speed. They are used to chase down and capture the high-speed boats used by drug smugglers in the Caribbean Sea and along the west coast of the United States.

The smallest boats used by the Coast Guard are called Rigid Hull Inflatable Boats, or RHIs. RHIs are **fiberglass** boats with a deep V-shaped **hull**. Outboard gasoline engines power them. An inflatable tube that helps the boat stay afloat surrounds the hull. RHIs are used to enter hard-to-get-to areas, such as shallow waters and rocky inlets.

Lightships

Before 1985 the Coast Guard had lightships. Lightships are ships anchored in one place, with a bright flashing light that warns approaching ships not to enter dangerous areas. In November 1913, the Buffalo, New York, Lightship #82 sank in Lake Erie after springing a leak in a powerful storm. All six crew members were lost. Later, the boat was recovered from the bottom of the lake and converted into a tender (boat that carries messages between shore and a larger ship).

Coast Guard Aircraft

The Coast Guard has more than 200 aircraft, including **helicopters** and **fixed-wing aircraft**, such as jets and **turboprops**. Aircraft are flown for search-and-rescue missions, law enforcement, and to help with environmental protection, such as monitoring oil spills.

The HC-130 Hercules is a long-range turboprop that is used for many kinds of **surveillance** and transport missions. The HU-25 Guardian jet is a medium-range surveillance aircraft.

Helicopters

Since the 1940s, helicopters have been used in Coast Guard air and water operations. The armed MH-68A Shark **helicopter** has been used to capture drug smugglers trying to reach the United States coastline in speedboats. None of the helicopters used by the Coast Guard today can perform water landings. However, they can take off from the flight decks of **cutters**.

Fastest Coast Guard Aircraft

The HU-25C Guardian jet is the fastest of all Coast Guard aircraft. It is almost twice as fast as any other, allowing it to arrive quickly at disaster scenes. It can reach speeds of 437 miles (703 kilometers) per hour.

An HC-25C Guardian flies over the California coast.

The Prinsendam Rescue

One of the greatest rescue missions in which the United States Coast Guard took part happened in 1980. On October 4 a fire broke out in the engine room of the cruise ship *Prinsendam*. At the time, it was located about 200 miles (322 kilometers) off shore in the Gulf of Alaska. The first message that the ship needed help was heard at about 1 A.M. Within ten minutes, the Coast Guard had a C-130 airplane and an HH-3F Pelican helicopter in the air. Three cutters were also sent to help. The Coast Guard had some help from the U.S. Air Force and Canadian forces. In about 24 hours, all 524 passengers and 200 crew were rescued. The fire raged on and the *Prinsendam* sank on October 11.

An MH-68A Shark helicopter participates in a training exercise.

Capturing drug smugglers

Coast Guard helicopters play a major role in capturing drug smugglers. Such captures usually involve the Coast Guard's MH-68A helicopters, also known as Sharks. These aircraft can travel up to 200 miles (322 kilometers) per hour. That is faster than almost any speedboat. The helicopters are armed with large rifles that can destroy the motor on a smuggler's boat.

The Last Amphibious Helicopter

The HH-3F Pelican was the last of the Coast Guard's **amphibious** helicopters. It was retired in 1994. Its retirement marked the end of the Coast Guard's "amphibious era." There were no more aircraft capable of making water landings.

Exciting Firsts in Coast Guard History

On the morning of December 17, 1903, Orville and Wilbur Wright completed the world's first airplane flight at Kitty Hawk, North Carolina. The event took place at the United States Coast Guard's Kill Devil Hills Life Saving Station. Three Coast Guard members carried the plane to its takeoff position. One of them took the only photograph of the event.

The Wright plane lifts off from the launching strip. Wilbur Wright ran alongside until the plane took off.

The first time the Coast Guard employed aircraft to seize a boat occurred on June 24, 1925. The plane had been borrowed from the navy. The plane flew at a top speed of 122 miles (196 kilometers) per hour. It could not fly any farther than 365 miles (587 kilometers) from the airbase before it had to turn around and return. The target was a boat being used to smuggle whiskey. This was during Prohibition (1920–1933), when the production and sale of alcoholic drinks were not allowed.

First African-American Commander

In 1928 Clarence Samuels became the first African American to command a Coast Guard vessel. Samuels was born in 1900 in Panama. When he first enlisted in the Coast Guard in 1920, he was not yet an American citizen. He served on the U.S. Coast Guard **cutter** *Sea Cloud* from August 1943 until July 1944. Clarence Samuels's career in the Coast Guard lasted twenty-seven years.

In 1943 the Coast Guard cutter *Sea Cloud* became the first United States military vessel to sail with a racially **integrated** crew. It patrolled in the North Atlantic, where it sank a German submarine. The *Sea Cloud* became a model for integrating the armed forces.

On January 15, 1947, the first **helicopter** to land at a base called Little America in Antarctica was from the U.S. Coast Guard. Pilot Lieutenant James A. Cornish had taken off from the icebreaker *Northwind*. He was part of Operation High-Jump, which was a mission led by the navy to explore Antarctica.

In 1977 Janna Lambine became the first female Coast Guard aviator. She was first assigned to a helicopter base. Some of her missions were search-and-rescue. Other times she flew **surveillance** missions to monitor water pollution and who might be doing it.

In 2001 Commander Sharon Donald-Baynes became the first African-American woman to command an operations ashore unit. She took charge of the Group Lower Mississippi River, in Memphis, Tennessee.

First Cutter to Go Round the World

In 1960–1961, the Coast Guard cutter *Eastwind* became the first vessel of its type to travel all the way around the globe. It sailed from Boston, passed through the Panama Canal, crossed the Pacific Ocean on its way to New Zealand, and even stopped at a Coast Guard station in Antarctica. It returned to Boston by way of the Indian Ocean. The journey lasted more than six months.

The Coast Guard cutter *Eastwind* opens a channel in Antarctica in 1963.

Early Heroes of the Coast Guard

First Coast Guard Aviator

Elmer F. "Archie" Stone is one of the most famous Coast Guard members. Stone was the first Coast Guard officer to become an aviator. With Norman Hall, he introduced the idea of using aircraft for Coast Guard missions in 1915. Stone was the pilot and navigator in 1919 on the first flight across the Atlantic Ocean.

Elmer Stone climbs into the cockpit of a Grumman JF-2 V167.

First Coast Guard Helicopter Pilot

On December 20, 1943, Frank A. Erickson became the first Coast Guard **helicopter** pilot. On January 3, he made the service's first helicopter life saving mission. The navy destroyer USS *Turner* had been anchored outside New York harbor. Around six o'clock in the morning, there was an explosion on the ship. Many of the men suffered serious burns. They were rescued from the sinking ship by the Coast Guard and taken to a hospital. In a dangerous storm with high winds, driving snow, and sleet, Erickson delivered blood **plasma** from Manhattan, New York, to a hospital in Sandy Hook, New Jersey. His bravery and piloting skill saved the lives of many survivors.

A Filipino Hero

Florence Ebersole Smith Finch, an Asian American who became a Coast Guard SPAR during World War II, actually was a hero before she joined the service. Florence's father was an American soldier and her mother was Filipino. The Japanese took over the Philippines in 1942 and imprisoned Americans there. Florence avoided imprisonment by claiming that she was a Filipino citizen. She then began to smuggle food and medicine to the American prisoners. Her work was cut short, however, when she was captured and imprisoned. Five months into her sentence, American forces freed her. She returned to the United States and enlisted in the Coast Guard. After the war she was awarded the United States **Medal of Freedom**.

Florence Ebersole Smith Finch

Coast Guard Medal of Honor Winner

Signalman First Class Douglas Munro was the only Coast Guard member to be awarded the Medal of Honor. Munro was evacuating marines from behind enemy lines on Guadalcanal in 1942 when he was killed in action.

Hero at 19

In 1980 William Ray "Billy" Flores was less than a year out of Coast Guard **boot camp.** He was on board the cutter *Blackthorn* when it collided with the tanker *Capricorn* near Tampa Bay, Florida. He died saving the lives of crew members from both vessels. Flores was just 19 years old.

Signalman First Class Douglas Munro

The Coast Guard Helps Win the World Wars

Coast Guard in World War I

The United States entered World War I (1917–1918) after four United States ships were sunk during one week in the spring of 1917. To help fight the war at sea, the United States Navy placed 15 Coast Guard **cutters** with 5,200 officers and enlisted men on duty. Their job was to hunt enemy submarines and ships. The cutters patrolled European and United States waters, plus Bermuda, the Azores, the Caribbean Sea, and off the coast of Nova Scotia. Eventually, 8,835 Coast Guard members served.

During World War I, the Coast Guard protected the nation's security in harbors and along shorelines. About 1,700 ships departed safely from the **port** of New York alone. The ships carried $550 million worth of military arms, which helped the United States and its European allies win the war.

The Tampa Disaster

The Coast Guard cutter *Tampa* was torpedoed in the Bristol Channel in southwest Great Britain in September 1918. The entire 115-man crew was killed. This tragic incident was one of the war's major sea disasters.

The Coast Guard cutter *Tampa* sinks during World War I.

The Coast Guard cutter *Spencer* explodes a depth charge that sank a Nazi **U-boat** during World War II.

Coast Guard in World War II

During World War II (1939–1945), Coast Guard pilots flew missions to find weather stations and possible enemy airfields in remote Greenland. Pilots braved arctic storms to rescue soldiers from remote areas. Coast Guard vessels patrolled for enemy submarines. Coast Guard ships sank eleven submarines and Coast Guard aircraft destroyed one. The Coast Guard rescued more than 2,500 people from enemy torpedo attacks.

Know It

The Coast Guard was first managed by the Department of Transportation. During wars, the U.S. Navy took command. Even though the Coast Guard is now in the Department of Homeland Security, the navy still takes over during times of war.

In all, 241,093 Coast Guard members, including 10,000 women, served in World War II. They took part in more than 1,000 search-and-rescue missions.

The Coast Guard During the Korean and Vietnam Wars

The Coast Guard set up a Long Range Aid to **Navigation** (LORAN) station in South Korea in 1953 to provide navigation information for United Nations vessels and aircraft.

Twenty-two Coast Guard **cutters** conducted search-and-rescue missions throughout the Pacific Ocean during the Korean War (1950–1953). The Coast Guard set up weather stations in faraway areas. Weather reports provide important information for predicting where the enemy will move and for planning battles. Coast Guard cutters also served as **communications** relay sites. Coast Guard aircraft protected United Nations troops that were being flown across the Pacific Ocean to and from battle stations. More than 44,000 Coast Guard **personnel** served in the Korean War.

Training a Korean Coast Guard

In 1946 retired Coast Guard officers were hired as advisors to train a new Korean Coast Guard. This force eventually became South Korea's navy. In June 1950, when the Korean War began, the advisors were called back to the United States. They immediately went to work training United States Navy recruits.

The Coast Guard cutter *Spencer* stops a Vietnamese fishing boat in 1965.

Coast Guard actions in Vietnam

During the Vietnam War (1965–1973), the United States Navy did not have boats that could operate in shallow water. So twenty-six of the Coast Guard's 82-foot (8-meter) cutters assisted the navy. These cutters became known as Squadron One. They patrolled dangerous waters and attacked enemy boats. They seized ammunition and equipment on Vietnamese boats. Other Coast Guard squadrons were stationed in deep-water areas.

In 1970,the cutter *Sherman* was under the command of Coast Guard Captain Paul A. Lutz. On November 21 the *Sherman* sank a North Vietnamese enemy ship that was attempting to supply guns and ammunition for enemy troops in South Vietnam. When navy divers investigated the sunken ship the next day, they found enough ammunition to supply an entire army division.

The Sherman's Finest Act

In early December the *Sherman* had only one day left on its last patrol when Captain Lutz learned that there was a **cholera** outbreak in a nearby town. The ship's doctor and the chief hospital corpsman wanted to go to the village and give shots to the villagers to protect them from the disease. There were no American soldiers near the town to provide protection, but Captain Lutz finally agreed to let them go. Some of the people in line to get shots were Viet Cong (the enemy). Later, Captain Lutz said, "Possibly, this unselfish act by these two brave men was the finest contribution that *Sherman* made during our time in Vietnam."

The Coast Guard Heads for the Persian Gulf

During the first Persian Gulf War (1991), Coast Guard **personnel** directed security at United States coastal ports. Coast Guard **reservists** protected the shoreline and other water-based areas. They loaded explosives onto ships heading for the Persian Gulf. Coast Guard law enforcement teams searched Iraqi ships for arms and explosives. Four hundred Coast Guard members served.

Persian Gulf Oil Spills

In early 1991 Iraqi troops fired on oil wells in Kuwait. This caused huge oil spills in the Persian Gulf. To help with the cleanup, two Coast Guard HU-25A Falcon jets flew to the gulf. They had special **technology** that finds oil floating on water. The Falcons were able to identify almost all the oil in a 40,000-square-mile (103,000-square-kilometer) area of the Persian Gulf.

A Coast Guard gunner's mate (foreground) and a navy sonar technician inspect an Iraqi merchant vessel in 1991.

In 2003 the Coast Guard crew of the cutter *Walnut* replaced Iraqi buoys in the North Arabian Gulf to insure safe passage of ships.

Coast Guard in Operation Iraqi Freedom

In 2003 the Coast Guard was a great help in Operation Iraqi Freedom. Coast Guard **cutters** protected important seaports and oil drilling platforms in the Persian Gulf. They performed maintenance on Iraqi waterways to allow the movement of military, commercial, and **humanitarian** supplies. They escorted commercial shipments to the region and took control of prisoners of war.

Meanwhile, homeland security efforts were increased in the war against terrorism. As part of this effort, the number of Coast Guard patrols was increased. Reservists were called to **active duty**. The number of cutters monitoring the ships arriving and leaving United States ports was also increased. From fall 2001 to spring 2003, more than 3,000 air and sea patrols were conducted.

Mascots

Over the years, Coast Guard crews have adopted animals
as ship mascots. Some mascots have even been inducted
officially into the organization. They have service numbers
and **personnel** records. Some mascots are even assigned
ranks and awards. Cats and dogs are common mascots,
but at least one eagle and one goat have made the grade,
too. In 1910 a bear was mascot of the **cutter** *Thetis* serving
in the Bering Sea.

Sinbad

Sinbad was a Chief Petty Officer in the United States Coast
Guard. What is surprising about this fact is that Sinbad was a
dog! For eleven years, through World War II and until 1951,
Sinbad lived on board the *Campbell*. He spent his last years of
retirement at the Barnegat, New Jersey, Light Station.

Sinbad poses
with some of his
shipmates on the
cutter *Campbell*
in 1943.

Camouflage

Camouflage the cat patrolled an LST (Landing Ship Tank) manned by Coast Guard personnel in 1945. He chased Japanese tracer bullets as they zigged and zagged across the deck of his ship. His playfulness gave the crew something to smile about during dangerous times.

Bozo

Bozo, a mascot aboard a Coast Guard combat **cutter** in the Far North, chewed the captain's shoes. He was confined to the **brig** for conduct unbecoming a ship's mascot. When he saw a group going ashore for leave, he looked very sad. The captain gave in and let him go ashore with the rest of the crew.

A Bear

The mascot of the cutter *Thetis* around 1910 was a bear who was also a veteran of the Bering Sea patrol.

Pete

Pete was the mascot of an 83-foot (25-meter) cutter during World War II. He would jump into the water to chase the rope, bring the line onto the dock, and help secure the vessel.

The Lonely Life of the Lighthouse Keeper

Lighthouses are towerlike buildings located along shorelines. They feature bright, often flashing, lights that warn ships about entering dangerous waters. Before lighthouses were **automated**, lighthouse keepers lit oil lamps each evening at dusk and refueled them at midnight. Every morning they cleaned the lamps. The keepers stood watch and used bells and gongs to alert ships when there was so much fog that the lights could not be seen. Later, even explosives were used as warning sounds. Today all lighthouses have loud horns that can be heard 8 miles (12.8 kilometers) away.

Because many lighthouses are in remote areas, keepers spent a lot of time by themselves or with only their families for company. In addition to their regular duties, they cleaned and painted the lighthouses. Most lighthouse keepers were male, but there also were female keepers. During the 1800s and early 1900s, more than 150 women served as **civilian** lighthouse keepers.

Established in 1857, the Dungeness Lighthouse in Puget Sound, Washington, was **automated** in 1976.

Know It

The first lighthouse dates to 285 B.C. in Alexandria, Egypt. It was simply a fire on a hillside that sailors could see from their ships. The first lighthouse in the United States was built on Little Brewster Island near Boston harbor in 1716.

Ida Lewis of Rhode Island

In the late 1800s in Newport, Rhode Island, Ida Lewis took over the lighthouse duties from her ill father. She was only 15 years old. Every weekday she rowed a boat to the mainland to take her sisters and brothers to school and get supplies. She was a lighthouse keeper for 39 years.

During the 1900s, one by one, lighthouses became automated. By the 2000s, every lighthouse was automated. Each is operated by specially trained Coast Guard **personnel** called Automated Lighthouse Technicians.

An Aids to Navigation Team member looks at the light in the lighthouse at St.Marks, Florida.

Manuel Ferreira of Hawaii

Coast Guard member Manuel Ferreira of Maui, Hawaii, was keeper of seven lighthouses during his 39-year career that ended in 1946. In 1919 he saved the lives of the crew of a Japanese fishing boat when it ran aground. In 1923 he saved the crew of a schooner about to crash into a reef. He could not use his boat because the seas were too rough. But he would not give up. So he ran 3 miles (4.8 kilometers) to the nearest phone to call for help.

Guarding the Environment

A Coast Guard marine inspector checks a pressure valve on an oil tanker in Mobile, Alabama.

The United States Coast Guard's Marine Safety, Security, and Environmental Protection Program helps keep people safe and protects the environment in waterways and along shorelines. Through this program, people can learn the Coast Guard's rules of **navigation**. There are also rules about boat safety and security. These rules must be followed when in **port** and when out on the water.

Environmental protection rules can cover such things as no-wake zones. These are areas in waterways where boats must travel very slowly. A fast-moving boat causes a wake, or a large wave, as it moves through the water. This wave can erode the banks of the waterway and disturb underwater plants.

Ballast Hitchhiker

The European zebra mussel is a foreign species that has damaged boats and ships. It has also crowded out native wildlife in the United States. It arrived in U.S. waterways in ships' **ballast**. Between 1989 and 2000, almost $1 billion has been spent to try and control it.

There are also rules about ballast water management. Large ships have tanks that are filled with water from the harbor when they do not have any cargo on board. This ballast water weighs down the ship and makes it more stable. When the ship takes on cargo at another port, the ballast tanks are emptied. The ballast might contain pollution or organisms that could harm the environment.

Biggest United States Oil Spill

On March 24, 1989, the *Exxon Valdez*, a 987-foot (300-meter) tanker, crashed into a reef in Alaskan waters. The ship held an overloaded cargo of 53 million gallons (200 million liters) of oil. Eleven tanks ripped open. Almost 11 million gallons (41 million liters) of crude oil leaked into Prince William Sound. It was the biggest oil spill in U.S. history. Many animals died, and the beauty of Prince William Sound was damaged. Cleanup efforts by Exxon Corporation were too late. The Coast Guard did save the ship and its crew, but could not contain the oil spill even with help from other federal agencies.

After the *Exxon Valdez* oil spill, the Coast Guard made new, stronger rules for oil tankers and the people who operate them. One rule calls for stronger **hulls** on oil tankers. There is also better **communication** between vessel captains and the traffic centers along the waterways.

A Coast Guardsman checks an oil recovery mesh while others blast rocks and shoreline soaked with crude oil from the *Exxon Valdez*.

Meet the Coast Guard:
Interview with Lieutenant Wes Hester

Lieutenant Wes Hester is a Coast Guard HC-130 (a **fixed-wing aircraft**) pilot. He is also a Public Affairs Officer. "As a C-130 pilot, I am in charge of a seven- to nine-person crew of both men and women," he explains. "We fly search-and-rescue missions looking for people in danger on the sea. We also fly homeland security missions. These missions usually last six to ten hours, and we attempt to identify vessels entering our **ports**. Other missions include law enforcement, environmental protection, and disaster relief.

"For this duty, I went through two years of training. We train in a joint training squadron, with navy, Coast Guard, air force, and marines. This training is academically and physically intense and is designed to take someone who has never been in an airplane and turn them into an effective pilot."

Lieutenant Hester's work as a Public Affairs Officer is his second duty. "I work closely with television, radio, and print media to promote the missions of the Coast Guard as well as our people. Additionally, I serve as an internal information officer, spreading critical information to the people assigned to [my] air station. Education for this job is primarily on-the-job-training."

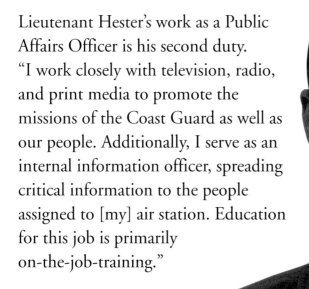

Lieutenant
Wes Hester

Lieutenant Hester stands at the door of his HC-130 **turboprop** aircraft.

Lieutenant Hester remembers his early days in the Coast Guard. "I joined the Coast Guard at seventeen years old. I enrolled in the United States Coast Guard Academy, located in New London, Connecticut. I chose aviation and went through flight school with the United States Navy.

"From day to day you never know what kind of mission you are going to fly. For the most part, we spend our days trying to save lives. It is the most rewarding form of work I could ever imagine."

Lieutenant Hester describes his most interesting mission: "A fishing boat sank 100 miles [161 kilometers] north of Bermuda. We launched out to find it. We located an electronic signaling beacon and searched for ten hours. We found debris from the vessel and called another C-130 out. The second C-130 found a man in the water floating on a piece of wood. They dropped a life raft out of the back of the plane, and the man crawled in and a passing ship saved him. The best part was he had survived on the piece of wood for sixteen hours!"

Meet the Coast Guard:
Interview with Petty Officer Jacquelyn Zettles

Jacquelyn Zettles is a first class petty officer in the United States Coast Guard. She is also a public affairs specialist at Coast Guard headquarters in Washington, D.C. She works as an editor and layout designer on *Coast Guard Magazine*, the official magazine of the Coast Guard.

"I was trained at the Defense Information School in Fort Meade, Maryland. I took a month-long class in editing and layout/design. We learned things like which way a picture should face on a page, how big headlines should be, and how to create balance on a page with color and white space. I earned my rank while doing my job. I've had great mentors and bosses to teach me the qualities of a good petty officer.

"I enlisted in the Coast Guard when I was twenty years old. I joined because I wanted a good environment to grow in my personal and professional life. I wanted to have adventures that would take me all across the world where I could meet new people and learn new things."

Petty Officer Jacquelyn Zettles chooses photographs for a new edition of *Coast Guard Magazine*.

Ready today, preparing for tomorrow

This *Coast Guard Magazine* was published in 2002.

Petty Officer Zettles thinks the Coast Guard is a wonderful career. "I think the Coast Guard is a great choice for young people who love the water, have an adventurous spirit, and like helping people. There are so many great jobs that can appeal to people with all different interests. One of the best times I had was shooting pictures from a **helicopter** in Hawaii. I took pictures of Coast Guard boats, lighthouses, and the endangered monk seal. The Coast Guard pilots opened the helicopter door, hooked me up to a gunner's belt, and let me shoot pictures from the door. Riding on that helicopter was like riding on a roller coaster. I had butterflies in my stomach the whole time!

"My job has trained me in journalism, photography, media relations, and digital imaging. . . . I have been in the Coast Guard for six years and I wouldn't trade a day of it. There have been many great days and some hard days, too, but no matter which one it was I always had wonderful people around to support me."

International Ice Patrol: The Polar Missions

The Coast Guard has operated the International Ice Patrol (IIP) since 1913. This group was formed after the *Titanic* hit an **iceberg** in April 1912 and sank. Seventeen nations have signed the treaty to participate in the IIP. The IIP watches for icebergs in the busy shipping lanes of the North Atlantic Ocean.

The IIP uses **fixed-wing aircraft** to patrol the region. A **radar** system helps them locate the icebergs. Each six-hour flight covers an area of about 30,000 square miles (77,000 square kilometers). That's as big as the state of Maine. The flights take place for five to seven days in a row, every two weeks.

Icebreakers

Icebreakers are **cutters** that are designed for crushing and breaking ice in open seas. They have extra-strong **hulls** and **bows** shaped especially for breaking up ice. The 399-foot (122-meter) *Polar Sea* and *Polar Star* travel through Arctic and Antarctic regions. These ships perform icebreaking duties and collect scientific data. They also carry supplies to remote research stations in the Antarctic.

Know It

The smallest icebergs are the size of small boats. They are more dangerous than large ones because often they are completely underwater. The two smallest types of icebergs are called growlers and bergy bits.

	Height (feet)	Height (meters)	Length (feet)	Length (meters)
Growler	less than 3	less than 1	less than 16	less than 5
Bergy Bit	3–13	1–4	15–46	5–14

The Coast Guard cutter *Polar Star* patrols in the west Arctic Sea.

The newest icebreaker

The *Healy* is the newest Coast Guard icebreaker. The Coast Guard began using it in 1999. The ship has a 4,200-square-foot (390-square-meter) scientific research laboratory. Fifty scientists can live on board at the same time. The *Healy* can break through 4.5 feet (1.37 meters) to almost 8 feet (2.43 meters) of ice. Like all icebreakers, the *Healy* is also involved with search-and-rescue. It also helps regular ships move safely through Arctic or Antarctic waters, helps with environmental protection, and enforces international marine laws and treaties.

Largest Iceberg

In 1956 Coast Guard **personnel** patrolling the Ross Sea off the coast of Antarctica spotted the largest known iceberg. It was 208 miles (335 kilometers) long and 60 miles (97 kilometers) wide. It would take you three and one-half hours to drive from one end to the other!

Keeping the Great Lakes open

Since 1944 the Great Lakes have had their own icebreaker, the *Mackinaw*. This ship has worked hard to keep shipping lanes open. In 2000 Congress agreed to fund a new icebreaker for the Great Lakes. It will also be called the *Mackinaw*.

This is the Great Lakes icebreaker, the *Mackinaw*.

Rescue at Sea

One of the oldest and most well known roles of the United States Coast Guard is its Search and Rescue program (SAR). Shipwrecks are a common type of SAR operation. They are caused by bad weather, broken equipment, or human error. The vessels in trouble might be pleasure boats on a lake or huge freighters sinking in storms at sea.

For Search and Rescue operations, the Coast Guard often uses 36- and 44-foot (11- and 13.4-meter) Motor Lifeboats, various **cutters**, and aircraft. The type of equipment used depends on the kind of accident and where it has happened. A **communications** network links all of the vehicles used. This allows crews on each boat or aircraft to receive up-to-date information.

Know It

The first time a U.S. Coast Guard cutter went to the rescue of people at sea was 1831.

A Coast Guard **helicopter** crew lowers a crew member to a boat under way.

The Coast Guard has a new 47-foot (14.3-meter) Motor Lifeboat that is built to take on 70-foot (21.3-meter) waves. It has room for a four-person crew. The cabin is airtight. This boat can be completely underwater upside down and will automatically (with no help from the crew) right itself. Then it will begin to bail (remove water) itself out within eight seconds.

A Coast Guard 47-foot Motor Lifeboat tops a wave in northwest Pacific Ocean surf. Such surf drills prepare crews for rescues in high seas.

Total Numbers for a Year

Each year the U.S. Coast Guard receives about 40,000 emergency calls. Coast Guard **personnel** save 4,000 or more lives each year. They also help at least 100,000 more people. But the Coast Guard works hard to prevent accidents from ever happening in the first place. Each year they perform safety inspections on 34,000 U.S.-controlled ships, boats, and barges. They also inspect 19,000 foreign-owned vessels for safety purposes.

Flags

The United States Coast Guard has two flags. One is called the ensign and the other is called the standard. An ensign shows that the ship or military group displaying it has a certain kind of authority. The standard identifies the group or organization.

The ensign was first flown in 1799 by order of the United States Congress. It was used on ships of the **Revenue Cutter** Service, which later became part of the Coast Guard. The service had to make sure that people did not smuggle goods into the new United States without paying taxes. When people saw this flag, they knew that the ship was not a pirate ship. The flag allowed the service to approach merchant ships safely.

Know It

The ensign must be flown whenever a Coast Guard vessel is on a law enforcement mission. It is never used in parades.

United States coat of arms

The Coast Guard ensign was designed by Oliver Wolcott in 1799.

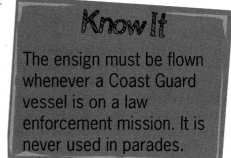

U.S. Coast Guard badge

The Ensign

In the original version, there were thirteen stars in a curved line above the eagle, thirteen leaves on the olive branch, thirteen arrows, and thirteen bars. These represented the thirteen states that existed when the United States was established. In this version the sixteen stripes represent the number of states when the ensign was first used. In 1951 the coat of arms was changed to match the one on the Great Seal of the United States.

The Coast Guard standard

The United States Coast Guard standard also has the United States coat of arms. Below it is the Coast Guard motto. The year 1790 is when the first agency of the Coast Guard was established. This flag is used in ceremonies and parades.

The color *red* on the flags stands for the United States' youth and the blood spilled in the war for freedom. The color *blue* is for justice and the nation's fight against oppression (the cruel power of authority). The color *white* stands for light and purity (not having any faults).

The Coast Guard standard is presented in New Jersey during a tribute to victims and heroes of 9/11.

The Corsair Fleet

During World War II (1941–1945), the Coast Guard formed the Temporary Reserves. About 2,000 sailing and motorboats were used. They patrolled coasts and watched for enemy submarines. This group was called the Corsair **Fleet**. Their logo, or symbol, was designed by Walt Disney Studios and shows a cartoon of Donald Duck costumed as a pirate complete with eyepatch, head scarf, and a sword.

A Visit to a United States Coast Guard Museum

The United States Coast Guard Museum is located on the grounds of the Coast Guard Academy, in New London, Connecticut. The museum displays items from the 200-year history of the Coast Guard. These include models of **cutters** and Inuit whale boats and kayaks, medals, uniforms, models of recruiting posters, and more.

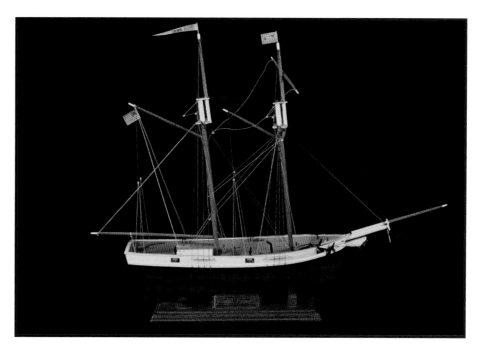

A model of the U.S. Revenue Cutter *Massachusetts*, one of the first ten cutters built, is on view at the Coast Guard Museum in New London.

Visitors can view cannons and memorials in a park and watch the Corps of Cadets march in formation. They also can board the Coast Guard training vessel, the *Eagle*. However, during times of war or increased security, people cannot visit the museum. This is because the Coast Guard Academy is off-limits to the public at these times.

"The Life-Boat Game"

One of the more unusual items on display at the Coast Guard Museum is The Life-boat Game, a children's board game produced by the Parker Brothers game company between 1899 and 1904.

The Coast Guard Museum Northwest is in Seattle, Washington. This museum also has thousands of Coast Guard items on display. Among the displays are a Lighthouse Service clock from 1860 and a flag that was in the first space shuttle in 1981. There is also a **navigation** instrument from a German submarine that the Coast Guard captured during World War II.

A visit to either museum will help you learn about the United States Coast Guard's history and people.

Coast Guard in Hollywood Films

During World War II, Hollywood often made films to show support for the people protecting the country. The Coast Guard Museum displays posters from several of these films. One is *Don Winslow of the Coast Guard* (1943), a 13-part series about a Coast Guard member who fights fictional Japanese invaders along the California coast.

Lighthouses to Visit

Many lighthouses have been taken over by local and state historical associations. People can visit the museums, which contain objects about the lighthouse. Usually they can also climb to the top of the lighthouses for more complete views of the area. Keepers are on hand to offer information.

The lighthouse at Portland Head, Maine, still works.

Glossary

active duty serving in the service on a full-time basis

amphibious operates on land and sea

automated operates or works by itself wit no help from a person

auxiliary additional

ballast weight on a ship that makes it more stable in the water

boot camp place where new members of the armed forces are trained

bow front end of a ship

brig jail on a ship

cholera type of infectious disease

civilian person who is not a member of the armed forces

commission give power to someone to perform certain duties. In the armed forces, officers receive documents that are their commissions.

communications sharing information

cutter Coast Guard vessel 65 feet (19.8 meters) in length or greater, with adequate living space for crew

data information

enlistee person who volunteers to serve in an armed force

fiberglass lightweight, strong material that combines plastic and glass

fixed-wing aircraft aircraft with wings that permanently attached to the body of the craft

fleet organized group of ships or boats

helicopter rotary-wing aircraft that can take off and land vertically

hull hollow, lower part of a ship that is in the water

humanitarian promoting human well-being

iceberg huge mass of ice that has broken free of glaciers or ice shelves

integrated brought together or combined

maritime of the sea, relating to shipping and navigation

Medal of Freedom highest presidential award for civilians

navigation science of getting ships, aircraft, or spacecraft from one place to another

personnel people who work for an organization such as the armed forces or a private business

plasma liquid part of blood separated from other elements

port place where ships dock

radar device used to find objects such as aircraft

recruits new members of the armed forces

reservists members of the armed forces who are not on active duty

revenue money earned by a government from taxes

revenue cutter ship used by the Coast Guard in the 18th and early 19th centuries to enforce customs regulations

stern back end of a ship

surveillance keep close watch over someone or something

technology applying science for practical purposes

turboprop aircraft with one or more propellers driven by a turbine jet engine

U-boat German submarine

More Books to Read

Gaines, Ann Graham. *The Coast Guard in Action.* Berkeley Heights, New Jersey: Enslow Publishers, 2001.

Holden, Henry M. *Coast Guard Rescue and Patrol Aircraft.* Berkeley Heights, New Jersey: Enslow Publishers, 2002.

Lyons, Lewis. *Rescue at Sea With the U.S. and Canadian Coast Guards.* Broomall, Penn.: Mason Crest Publishers, 2003.

Weintraub, Aileen. *Life Inside the Coast Guard Academy.* Danbury, Conn.: Children's Press, 2002.

Official Coast Guard Website

www.uscg.mil/USCG.shtm
Gives information about the Coast Guard, its services, history, and equipment such as aircraft and cutters, plus its various missions.

Index

United States Coast Guard

Lurch, Bruno
ATOS BL 6.9
Points: 1.0   MG